The INSIDE GUIDE

CELEBRATING NATIVE AMERICAN CULTURES

Native American Celebrations and Ceremonies

By Trisha James

Cavendish Square

New York

Published in 2023 by Cavendish Square Publishing, LLC
29 E. 21st Street New York, NY 10010

Website: cavendishsq.com

This publication represents the opinions and views of the author based on their personal experience, knowledge, and research. The information in this book serves as a general guide only. The author and publisher have used their best efforts in preparing this book and disclaim liability rising directly or indirectly from the use and application of this book.

Disclaimer: Portions of this work were originally authored by Kate Mikoley and published as *Native American Celebrations and Ceremonies: From Potlatches to Powwows* (Native American Cultures). All new material this edition authored by Trisha James.

All websites were available and accurate when this book was sent to press.

Cataloging-in-Publication Data

Names: James, Trisha.
Title: Native American celebrations and ceremonies / Trisha James.
Description: New York : Cavendish Square Publishing, 2023. | Series: The inside guide: celebrating Native American cultures | Includes glossary and index.Identifiers: ISBN 9781502664242 (pbk.) | ISBN 9781502664266 (library bound) | ISBN 9781502664259 (6pack) | ISBN 9781502664273 (ebook) Subjects: LCSH: Indians of North America–Rites and ceremonies–Juvenile literature. | Indians of North America–Social life and customs–Juvenile literature. Classification: LCC E98.R53 J36 2023 | DDC 970.004'97–dc23

Editor: Therese Shea
Copyeditor: Jill Keppeler
Designer: Deanna Paternostro

Find us on

CONTENTS

Chapter One: 5

Unique Peoples, Unique Rituals

Chapter Two: 11

Sacred Ceremonies

Chapter Three: 17

The Potlatch and Other Community Rituals

Chapter Four: 23

Healing, Harmony, and History

More to Explore   28

Think About It!   29

Glossary   30

Find Out More   31

Index   32

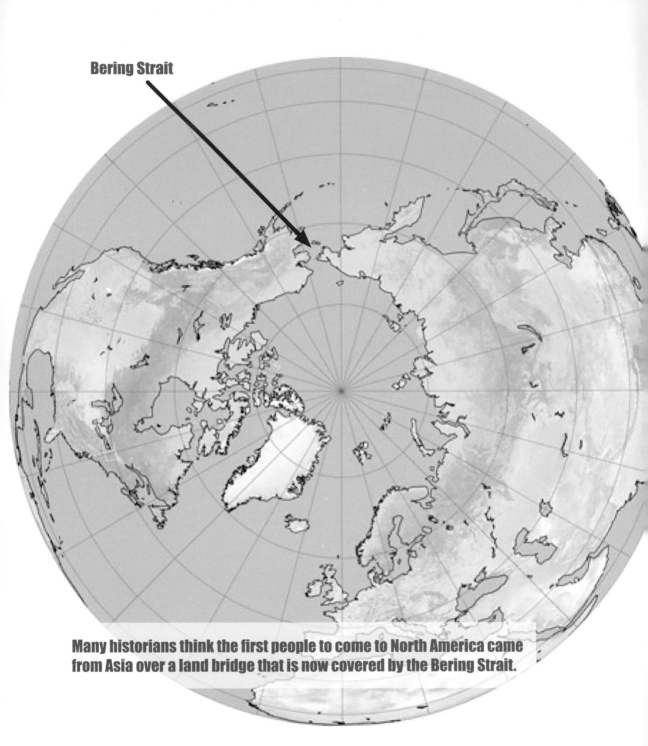

Bering Strait

Many historians think the first people to come to North America came from Asia over a land bridge that is now covered by the Bering Strait.

Chapter One

UNIQUE PEOPLES, UNIQUE RITUALS

The first people to live in a place are called Indigenous people. Native Americans are the Indigenous peoples of the Americas. They lived there long before the countries of the United States, Canada, Mexico, and the many nations of Central and South America were founded. They were in these areas thousands of years before Europeans arrived to explore and settle the land.

The many **cultures** of Native Americans, past and present, are full of unique, or one-of-a-kind, traditions. Their ceremonies and celebrations are often deeply based in **spirituality** as well as a respect for **ancestors** and the natural world. Perhaps the most well known of Native American **rituals** today is the powwow.

Fast Fact

Asia and North America remained connected by land until about 12,000 years ago. Now, this area is covered by the Bering Strait.

The Powwow

The powwow is an event in which people, often from several Native American nations, come together to dance, sing, and honor the traditions of the past. The word once meant something different, though. It comes from *pau wau*,

COUNTING NATIVE AMERICANS

Every 10 years, the U.S. government carries out a census of the nation. A census is a count of the population, but it also collects information about the people, including age, sex, race, and location. The 2010 census reported that the "American Indian and Alaska Native population" in the country numbered about 5.2 million. In 2020, this number ballooned to 9.7 million. This includes people who say they are Native American alone as well as those who are Native American as well as other races. Why such a large increase? It could be because people are becoming more aware and accepting of their ancestry. Plus, Native Americans have been undercounted in the past.

Fast Fact

The Indigenous peoples of North America are most often called Native Americans, American Indians, and First Peoples (especially in Canada). While this book mostly uses "Native American," different communities prefer different terms.

which means "medicine man" in the **Algonquian** language called Narrtick, spoken by Native peoples in what's now Massachusetts. British settlers used the word to mean a meeting of medicine men or spiritual leaders, and later any meeting of Native Americans.

Traveling European merchants used the word "powwow" for medicines they sold, and they sometimes paid Native Americans to dance during "medicine shows" used to attract people

Modern powwows are different from the ceremonies of the early Native Americans, but they're rooted in many of the same traditions.

to buy their goods. Finally, Native Americans adopted the word "powwow" themselves to mean any dancing **exhibition** they might put on for an audience. Gatherings similar to powwows have existed in most Native American communities since long before Europeans came to North America.

A Changing Event

In the 19th and 20th centuries, the U.S. government tried to stop Native Americans from practicing many of their traditions. They wanted them to **assimilate** into white American culture. This meant giving up hunting for some and even sending their children away to schools where they had to speak English and dress and act in ways different from their people's traditional ways of life. Some rituals were lost during this period. However, the powwow survived. Its features have changed over the years, but its meaning and importance remains.

Powwows today can last anywhere from one to four days. Dancers, singers, and artists from hundreds of miles away may attend these community gatherings. Most powwows are open to the public. Some offer prize money for dance and music contests. People travel all over the country to compete at powwows and connect with friends of different cultures.

The songs and dances at modern powwows often come from the traditions of Plains peoples, such as the Omaha and Ponca.

The Hopi have maintained their rich cultural traditions over the years, including ceremonies like the Snake Dance and arts such as basket weaving, shown below.

Chapter Two

SACRED CEREMONIES

Just as in many cultures, some Native American ceremonies and traditions stem from Native American religions. Native American religions are complex and often can't be easily described. In fact, some Native Americans might not even call their spiritual practices a religion but rather a way of life that touches on every part of their culture. Sacred ceremonies are equally as complex and can only be fully understood by the Native peoples who practice them.

Fast Fact

Benjamin Nuvamsa, former chairman of the Hopi Tribe, said, "The practitioners of these very sacred ceremonies are forbidden to divulge [tell] to anyone, even other Hopis, the most esoteric [secret] details of the ceremonies."

The Snake Dance

The Hopi were the group of Plains peoples who lived farthest west, in today's northeastern Arizona. The Hopi Tribe still lives there today. Arizona is often hot and dry, so certain Hopi ceremonies ask gods and spirits for rain for their crops.

Part of one Hopi ceremony, the Snake Dance, was once open for the public to see. During the 16-day event, often in August, the Hopi gathered snakes and prepared them for the ritual. Some danced with the snakes in their mouths. Finally, the snakes were let go in all directions to carry prayers for rain to the gods. The Snake Dance was also a way to give thanks and ask for overall good fortune.

Outsiders were fascinated by this ceremony, but the Hopi began to believe that photographs, drawings, and even the presence of outsiders was having a **negative** effect on this ritual. Outsiders sometimes talked about it in a disrespectful way. The Hopi finally forbid the public from viewing the Snake Dance.

The Sun Dance

Different forms of the ceremony called the Sun Dance exist throughout Native American cultures. It served different purposes for different peoples. For most, it was a way to connect with ancestors, nature, and each other.

For the Sun Dance of the Plains peoples, Native Americans gathered for several days in late spring or in early summer. Sometimes people also danced in the time leading up to the Sun Dance. For the Sun Dance itself, only certain people who had prepared themselves for months took part with the support of the community. The dancers began at a certain time and continued their movements with few breaks throughout several days and nights. They didn't eat food or drink water during this time. Though they grew weak

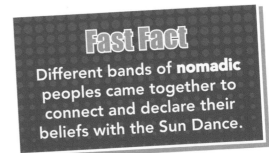

Fast Fact

Different bands of **nomadic** peoples came together to connect and declare their beliefs with the Sun Dance.

A GREAT HONOR

In 1913, former U.S. president Theodore Roosevelt watched the Snake Dance at a time when outsiders were still allowed to attend. He later said, "There were hundreds of onlookers the day we were there. Many of the tourists did not show the proper respect for the religious observance they were watching." Roosevelt credited his respectful manner with why he was allowed to observe the most sacred preparations for the dance. He was even invited into a kiva, an underground room, which was unusual for an outsider. He admired both the Snake Dance and the Hopi people's customs.

This is a reconstruction of a kiva at Mesa Verde National Park in Colorado, where **Ancestral Pueblo** people lived.

Fast Fact

Some Sun Dance participants were pierced with needles and connected to the center pole through the piercing.

physically, they believed they gathered spiritual power and boosted their people's well-being.

In 1883, the United States made doing the Sun Dance illegal. It remained that way until 1934. Even during that time, forms of the ritual continued, and they survive to this day. The tradition is practiced on the **reservation** of the Blackfeet Nation in Montana, for example.

Some Native American communities centered the Sun Dance around a tall pole, symbolizing their connection to a god or the sun.

15

Sometimes the host of a potlatch gifted the right to wear special clothing. This Tlingit woman wears potlatch ceremonial dress.

THE POTLATCH AND OTHER COMMUNITY RITUALS

Certain life events called for a community gathering in most Native American groups. A potlatch was one such gathering among Native Americans of the Pacific Northwest. Traditionally, potlatches were given in honor of marriages, births, and deaths. One person invited a number of community members. The gathering included music, speeches, dancing, and gifts. Gifts were given to the people who attended according to each person's social status in the community. The more the host gave away, the greater their own social rank in the community.

Potlatches were also a way for rivals to try to outdo each other or for someone who had suffered public shame or embarrassment to regain good standing. Modern potlatches are most often held to honor an important person after their death. Potlatches can last for several days and take years to prepare for.

The Kwakwaka'wakw people, who continue to celebrate the potlatch, describe the gathering as a time of pride and joy. Elder Agnes Axu Alfred explained, "When one's heart is glad,

Fast Fact

Potlatch hosts gave property as gifts as well as the right to sing certain songs, tell certain stories, or dance certain dances. They also gave money, food, and clothing.

POTLATCH BAN

In the late 19th century, the potlatch was banned in both the United States and Canada in an effort to make Native peoples assimilate. Some **defiant** Indigenous peoples, knowing the importance of the practice to their culture, refused to stop. In 1921, Dan Cranmer, a chief of the 'Na̲mgis Nation, held the largest potlatch recorded on the British Columbia coast in Canada. Dozens of people were arrested for taking part. Some spent months in prison. A government agent took many of the potlatch gifts and even charged outsiders a fee to see them. They were later given to a museum. The ban on potlatches ended in the United States in 1934 and in Canada in 1951.

he gives away gifts. Our Creator gave it to us, to be our way of doing things, to be our way of rejoicing … Everyone on earth is given something. The potlatch was given to us to be our way of expressing joy."

The Green Corn Ceremony

Many cultures around the world have ceremonies to celebrate the first harvest, or crop, of the year. The Green Corn Ceremony was one such celebration in many Native American communities, especially those indigenous to the Southeast such as the Choctaw and the Seminole.

Ceremonies differ depending on the group, but they often feature prayers, dancing, and games. For the Seminole, this was also a time to

Fast Fact

In 1830, the Choctaw were forced to give the United States their territory in the Southeast and were given land in the Indian Territory (now Oklahoma) in exchange.

settle disagreements. Thanks are given to the gods for the rain, sun, corn, and other crops. Fasting, or not eating for a period of time, was part of the ceremony for the Choctaw, whose sacred ceremony was four days long.

These are images from the Green Corn Native American Festival and Powwow in Tennessee in 2021.

The Green Corn Ceremony has been **revived** by the Choctaw Nation of Oklahoma. The Seminole of south Florida still observe the Green Corn Ceremony too. It isn't open to the public, however.

The First Laugh Ceremony

In the Navajo community, a baby's first laugh is a significant event. Some believe the laugh means the baby has left the spiritual world and is now fully in the physical world with their family. A feast is given to honor the occasion, often within four days of the laugh.

The baby is considered the host of the celebration. However, the person who made the baby laugh is often in charge of preparing for it.

Fast Fact
The person putting on the First Laugh ceremony helps the baby give guests gifts of rock salt, which is a reminder of the Navajo people's connection to the earth.

In the Navajo tradition, children belong to the world of the Holy People. Laughter is a sign they're ready to live with their earthly family.

The Haudenosaunee were largely located in and around present-day New York State. A Haudenosaunee man is shown here dancing at the New York State Fair.

HEALING, HARMONY, AND HISTORY

Many Indigenous peoples of North America had societies focused on healing. Sometimes called medicine societies or curing societies, these groups practiced rituals to restore the well-being of both individuals and the community. One of the best known of these societies was the False Face Society of the Haudenosaunee (sometimes called the Iroquois) of the Northeast.

False Face Society members carved wooden masks from trees. The masks were considered to be living spirits when cared for correctly. False Face ceremonies included chants, or song-prayers, and dances to drive out illness and bad luck. Haudenosaunee who were cured by the False Face Society became a part of it.

False Face masks were once found in museums and pictured in books, but in the early 2000s, many Native American groups requested that they not be shown in public anymore, out of respect for sacred beliefs.

Fast Fact

The most famous medicine society among the Upper Great Lakes Algonquians was the Midewiwin, or Grand Medicine Society.

The Blessingway

The Navajo have many healing ceremonies too. The Blessingway is a series of chants that promote health, harmony, and success. While the Blessingway isn't meant to cure sickness, it's used to bring blessings and prevent bad luck. Pieces of the Blessingway are included in most Navajo ceremonies.

Fast Fact

The Navajo, the largest group of Native Americans in the United States as of 2021, live mostly in New Mexico, Arizona, and Utah.

The Blessingway usually lasts two nights, but it's sometimes part of longer ceremonies. Its chants speak of the first peoples and how they overcame evil. Sometimes the singer, often a male, uses a rattle during the Blessingway.

Navajo also create sandpaintings, or drypaintings, as part of the Blessingway ceremony. Sandpainting involves using colored sands to form designs on a flat surface. Sandpainting ceremonies are held only for Navajo people. Art may be based on a certain sandpainting design, but usually representations of Navajo gods are removed before such art is sold to members of the public.

Continuing Cultures

Today, many Native American peoples continue the rituals described in this book. Some remain on their traditional lands. Others are hundreds of miles away from the lands of their ancestors. Some follow traditional ways of life. Others live in cities and support themselves in ways much different than their ancestors did. By taking part in the ceremonies and

Navajo sandpainting is linked to healing rituals. The painting is destroyed after the ritual.

THE IÑUPIAT BLANKET TOSS

The Iñupiat are a Native people of northern Alaska. They mark the end of whale-hunting season with a celebration of thanks to the whales and the whale hunters. It includes prayers, songs, dancing, stories, and a blanket toss—called Nalukataq.

For the blanket toss, sometimes 30 or more men and women gather in a circle and hold the ends of a large blanket made of sealskin. Then, they take turns bouncing on it, at times reaching 40 feet (12 meters) in the air, and trying to land on their feet. Some do flips!

Fast Fact

The blanket toss may have begun as a way for hunters to spot animals from far away!

Powwows, often open to the public, may exhibit the dances, dress, chants, and songs of just one nation or many.

A large crowd watches the blanket toss at the Nalukataq whaling festival in Utqiagvik, Alaska.

celebrations of their **heritage**, Native Americans of all walks of life can stay connected to their culture and keep it alive for the next generation.

One of the best ways to learn more about an Indigenous people is to attend one of their cultural events that is open to the public. It's also an ideal way to show support and respect for the rich traditions of Native Americans.

Features of a Powwow

Grand Entry
  Native dancers parade into exhibition area, led by an **eagle staff**

Flag Song
  pays respect to the national flag

Master of Ceremonies/Announcers
  explain traditions to audience, direct dancers and drummers, tell jokes

Dancers
  different categories, including men's and women's fancy dance and men's and women's traditional, depends on region

Music
  provided by drummers and singers, northern or southern style

Judges
  score dancers and singers in different contests

Closing Ceremony
  elder says closing prayer, participants proceed out behind the eagle staff

THINK ABOUT IT!

1. Can you understand why certain Native American groups no longer allow outsiders to see their sacred ceremonies? Why or why not?

2. Why do you think the U.S. and Canadian governments thought banning certain celebrations and ceremonies, such as the potlatch, would be effective in forcing Native peoples to assimilate?

3. Some ceremonies have been revived in recent years. Why might Native peoples not be able to revive all their past customs?

4. Can you think of similarities between any of the celebrations in this book and those that your family celebrates? Explain.

Dancers at Potlatch, Chilkat, Alaska.

GLOSSARY

Algonquian: A widespread family of languages spoken by Indigenous peoples from the Atlantic Coast as far west as the Great Plains.

ancestor: A person in someone's family who lived in past times.

Ancestral Pueblo: The ancestors of the Pueblo peoples who once lived where the U.S. states of Arizona, New Mexico, Colorado, and Utah meet.

assimilate: To take on the culture of another group or groups.

culture: The beliefs and ways of life of a group of people.

defiant: Refusing to obey.

eagle staff: A symbol of a Native American nation that usually looks somewhat like a shepherd's staff and features eagle feathers.

exhibition: A public show of something such as art or skills.

heritage: The traditions and beliefs that are part of the history of a group or nation.

negative: Harmful or bad.

nomadic: Having to do with people who move from place to place.

reservation: Land set aside by the U.S. government for Native Americans to live on.

revive: To bring something back into use.

ritual: A formal ceremony.

spirituality: The quality or state of believing in spirits or gods.

FIND OUT MORE

Books

Grover, Kevin, and Wilma Mankiller. *Do All Indians Live in Tipis? Questions and Answers from the National Museum of the American Indian*. Washington, D.C.: Smithsonian Books, 2019.

O'Mara, John. *The Hopi*. New York, NY: Enslow Publishing, 2022.

Pheasant-Neganigwane, Karen. *Powwow: A Celebration Through Song and Dance*. Victoria, British Columbia: Orca Book Publishers, 2020.

Websites

Potlatch
umistapotlatch.ca/potlatch-eng.php
Learn about this kind of ceremonial party from the Kwakwaka'wakw people.

What Do Native Americans Celebrate?
www.bbc.co.uk/bitesize/articles/z36rvwx
Read about the Omaha people's celebrations as explained by a member of the nation.

INDEX

A
Alaska, 26, 27
Algonquians, 23
Arizona, 11, 24

B
Blackfeet, 14
Blessingway, 24

C
Choctaw, 18, 19, 20

F
False Face Society, 23
First Laugh ceremony, 20
Florida, 7, 20

G
Grand Medicine Society, 23
Green Corn Ceremony, 18, 19, 20

H
Haudenosaunee (Iroquois), 22, 23
Hopi, 10, 11, 12, 13

I
Iñupiat, 26

K
Kwakwaka'wakw, 17

M
Massachusetts, 6
Montana, 14

N
Nalukataq, 26, 27
'Namgis, 18
Navajo, 20, 24, 25
New Mexico, 24
New York (state), 22

O
Oklahoma, 19, 20
Omaha (people), 8

P
Plains peoples, 8, 11, 12
Ponca, 8
potlatch, 16, 17, 18, 29
powwows, 5, 6, 7, 8, 19, 26, 28

Pueblo peoples, 13

S
Seminole, 7, 18, 20
Snake Dance, 10, 11, 12, 13
Sun Dance, 12, 14, 15

T
Tlingit, 16

U
Utah, 24